Big Rigs for MOMS

A Crash Course in Sons for New Mothers

Jenna McCarthy

SASQUATCH BOOKS
SEATTLE

"I'm a Wizard, I'm a Warlock" is reprinted with permission from *My Hippo Has the Hiccups*, Kenn Nesbitt, published by Sourcebooks, Inc.

Printed in Canada
Published by Sasquatch Books
Distributed by PGW/Perseus
15 14 13 12 11 10   10 9 8 7 6 5 4 3 2 1

Cover and interior design: Rosebud Eustace
Cover and interior illustrations: Sasha Barr

Library of Congress Cataloging-in-Publication Data

McCarthy, Jenna.
 Big rigs for moms : a crash course in sons for new mothers / Jenna McCarthy.
     p. cm.
 ISBN 978-1-57061-622-8
 1. Mothers and sons—Humor. 2. Clothing and dress--Humor. I. Title.
 PN6231.M68M43 2010
 818'.607—dc22

                           2009039486

Sasquatch Books
119 South Main Street, Suite 400
Seattle, WA 98104
(206) 467-4300
www.sasquatchbooks.com
custserv@sasquatchbooks.com

Contents

Introduction

You felt you were totally prepared for motherhood and all of its joys and challenges. You read the recommended books. You spent months exercising gently but regularly, dutifully popped mountains of prenatal vitamins, and lovingly pre-washed an assortment of organic, gender-neutral onesies and receiving blankets. You were as ready as any expecting mom ever has been to assume her new role—that is, until you heard those three little words that have been known to strike fear into many a woman's heart:

It's a boy.

It's not that you *didn't* want a boy, or really had any preference one way or another. You wanted a healthy baby with 10 fingers and 10 toes. Pink or blue was utterly beside the point! And already you love your little mini-man with every atom in your being.

But still. Still there is a little voice in your head that keeps reminding you of a simple fact: you are a girl. Ergo, boys are a mystery. Even if you happen to be an oil-changing, tractor-driving, football-playing, fish-catching mom yourself, there are approximately a zillion things about being a boy you may know nothing about. Your son is likely to bombard you with questions about backhoes and baseball scores, semi trucks and slingshots. He'll fall asleep clutching a toy tank engine. He'll beg you to stop at every construction site you pass for the next 13 or so years. And guess what else, mom? It'll probably be *you* who makes the call on whether he learns to pee standing up or sitting down.

Don't be daunted! You'll still be able to enjoy elaborate tea parties together (if that's your thing), and—if he's like 99.9 percent of little guys out there—he'll love nothing more than clanking about the house in the highest heels you own. He'll probably fancy fairy wings and magic wands. He may even want his fingernails painted on occasion. (If you're inclined to indulge, we advise doing this when Dad's out of town for a few days.)

For all of those in-between times, think of this book as your manual of all things masculine. It will help you appreciate his need to turn every stick, hose, and toilet paper roll into a weapon, tell you how to explain the critical difference between a backhoe and an excavator, and allow you to confidently defend your position on just which historical pirate was actually the coolest.

The great news is that boys adore their mothers. You won't have to don anything fancy or sparkly to be beautiful in his eyes. And the first time he high-fives you for your killer dunk shot, your heart will melt on the spot. Help him master the same

move and he's guaranteed to turn into a puddle
too (at least on the inside).

All Aboard!

You may have fond but distant memories of that plucky little-engine-that-could, but beyond that, your knowledge of trains very well may be limited to the old "Open the tunnel—here comes the choo choo!" feeding-time routine. Time to step it up, Mom. Odds are your son is going to be fascinated by anything railway-related—and naturally he'll expect you to come along for the ride.

A word of warning: Googling "trains" will produce somewhere in the mind-numbing neighborhood of 52 million hits, many of them jam-packed with information about scary-sounding, rail-related thingamabobs like a lemprex ejector, wootten firebox, and the good old Krauss-Helmholtz bogie. (Yes, these are real things.) Clearly, trains are not for the faint of heart. But no one said you needed to know *every bloody thing* about them—a few key facts and some random trivia ought to get you on the right track.

Your first order of business will be to familiarize yourself with Thomas the Tank Engine. This will not be difficult, as you can barely turn your head in any toy store without bumping into this lively blue locomotive. (The good news: Thomas was the brainchild of the honorable Reverend W. Awdry, so you can be sure the stories promote good, whole-some fun—even if they can be a tad preachy at times.)

Fast, fun Thomas facts

- Thomas lives on the fictional Island of Sodor; his route was inspired by the Great Western Line from Paddington to Bristol, England.

(Sounds like an excuse to spring for a European family vacation!)

- The venerable reverend wrote one railway story a year until he published his 26th and final one (*Tramway Engines*) in 1972. The reverend's son and muse, Christopher, went on to pen an additional 14 train tales.

- From the page to prime time: *Thomas the Tank Engine & Friends* became a hit TV show soon after its launch in Britain in 1985. By 1989, Thomas had made his way to America, becoming a popular PBS staple. Today, Thomas has chugged across the small screen in 130 countries around the world.

- In 1985, former Beatles drummer Ringo Starr became the behind-the-scenes sound of the featured storyteller on the TV show's first two series. Other familiar voices followed, including George Carlin (in 1991), Alec Baldwin (in 1998), and the occasional guest appearance by Pierce Brosnan.

- Thomas has more than 40 friends—from affable Alfie to the disaster-prone duo known as the "Troublesome Trucks." You can find a list on www.thomasandfriends.com; book-mark it now because your little guy is bound to be begging you to log on before you know it.

Train terms for dummies

Although your child may be able to point out every sub-category of train car in existence, all can be divided into four primary categories:

- **COACHES:** cars that carry passengers

- **TANKERS:** cars that carry liquids

- **TENDERS:** cars that carry the train's fuel and water

- **WAGONS:** cars that carry freight, also referred to as freight cars

Random trivia to impress your little conductor

- Legend has it that the phrase "the real McCoy" was a tribute to Elijah McCoy, the Canadian inventor who patented the first successful machine used to lubricate train engines.

- According to FunTrivia.com, Mallard No. 4468 set a record for its supersonic speed of 126 mph on July 3, 1938. It was pulling seven coaches.

- Australia's BHP Iron Ore is considered the longest train in history with 682 cars. (Imagine waiting for *that* one when you're late for a dentist appointment. D'oh!)

Come Clean

You may go through flaming hoops to keep yourself, your home, your car, and the majority of your possessions looking polished and pretty—but if your little boy had his way, the world would be one giant pigpen. The more dirt, the better! Throw in some water and he's in hog heaven.

Why the fascination with filth? It's fun! Its potential is limitless. And it's just so darned *dirty*. What's not to love? Sure there are plenty of little girls who'll spend hours digging for worms or making sand castles—but whereas this is likely more of a specific, isolated activity for her, he'll find a way to get filthy doing just about anything. "How did he get so grimy playing *cards*?" you'll wonder, reaching for the three-gallon bottle of stain remover.

Since you can't beat 'em (remember, this is the kid who's going to demand a *dirt bike* some day in the not-too-distant future), you might as well join 'em. Obviously, making mud pies in the living room is out of the question. Ideally, you have space out-side to create a designated dirt zone. A sandbox, for instance, is a wise investment as he'll enjoy burrowing in it for many years to come. If you live in an apartment, a small one on a patio or bal-cony can help satisfy his urge to excavate. (Make sure to buy or craft some sort of cover for it, as every neighborhood cat, squirrel, skunk, raccoon, mouse, and other assorted vermin will waste no time christening their enormous new litter box.) In a pinch, a few old kitchen bowls, funnels, mea-suring cups, and plastic containers, combined with some simple dirt or gravel and water, might be enough to entertain your boy long enough for you to enjoy a cup of coffee and a personal phone call. Maybe mud isn't so bad after all!

Ideas for winning the grime game

- Got a garden? Turn your dirt-lover into a budding botanist. Teach him which plants are weeds and put him to work. Give him a small spade and a packet of seeds and suddenly destruction is constructive. You might also designate a single garden pot to your child, decorate it with his name, and put him in charge of planting, watering, and maintaining it. Don't forget daily insect checks!

- Head to the beach or playground with a bucket of small toys, plastic coins, and other riches, and ask him to cover his eyes while you hide them. He'll spend hours searching for the buried treasure. (Just don't let him get his hands on your keys, or this game could become interminable. Literally.)

- Designate a Dirt Day and let him try to get as grubby as possible. Take pictures of his progress throughout the day and reward him with a long bubble bath before bed. This could satisfy his dirt-urges for the next few days.

- As he isn't naturally inclined to notice that his shoes, hands, and hair are all caked with crumbling mud, consider instituting a rule where nobody goes into the house after outside play without being body-checked by Mom first. Or, weather-permitting, allow him to strip down to skivvies before reentering the house.

- Still sitting on the sidelines? Roll up your sleeves and get in there! Take turns burying each other's feet and then busting out, going on a worm hunt, or racing to see who can dig the biggest hole. Winner gets to hose the other one down first.

(Little) Men at Work

If there comes a day when you can't quite grasp your son's fascination with buildings-in-process, try to look at it through *his* eyes: construction sites are loud. They're dirty. They're deliciously dangerous. They have trucks! Sometimes, there's even a *food* truck stationed right on site—one that sells such exotic delicacies as pink coconut donuts and batter-fried taquitos. (You might fascinate your son by explaining that this kind of meals-on-wheels contraption is commonly and disconcertingly referred to as the "roach coach.") Best of all, construction sites are frequently popu-lated by macho, muscled dudes toting mysterious, heavy tools and muttering all manner of exciting new obscenities.*

Even if you can't tell a two-by-four from a sheet of plywood, your budding builder may soon be quiz-zing you on an assortment of construction tools and machinery—many of which look practically identical. These helpful charts will help you talk construction as confidently and convincingly as Bob the Builder (who you will soon get to know intimately).

*For the last reason in particular, construction sites are often best perused from the car with the windows rolled up. You won't always be able to pull this off, but don't say you weren't warned.

The vehicle	What it looks like	What it does
backhoe	a tractor with hinged, bucket-like jaws	lifts and moves large chunks of earth and debris
forklift	a tractor with an L-shaped lift on the front	slides under large boxes/palates to lift and move them
excavator	a tractor with a huge, booming ladle arm	digs, moves, and deposits loose dirt and gravel
crane	a truck with a telescoping ladder on top	lifts crews and materials to great heights
cement mixer	a truck with a large, revolving barrel	maintains the liquid state of cement or concrete for transporting to the construction site
dump truck	a large, long truck with an open, hinged bed	transports and deposits loose materials such as sand, gravel, or dirt
bulldozer	any size tractor with belt-like wheels and a large front plate	moves large amounts of dirt or debris

The vehicle	What it looks like	What it does
roller	a tractor that drags a long cylinder behind it	used to level, crush, or smooth a surface
cherry picker	a truck with a basket or cage attached to the top of a moveable boom	lifts workers up to build or repair at great heights . . . or of course, pick cherries

The tool	What it looks like	What it does
band saw	two wheels with a poky saw revolving around them (imagine a bike chain with spikes)	cuts metal, dense wood, and other impossibly hard materials
jig saw	an electric turkey carving knife with a narrow blade	cuts curves and other difficult lines and patterns
drill	a hand-held electric gun with a twisty, rotating point (known as a "bit")	makes holes in things
table saw	a circular saw mounted under a table or bench with the blade poking up through a slot	cuts a straight line through wood, drywall, or other materials
level	a fat, 3-D ruler with bubbles inside it	allows you to determine if something is perfectly horizontal or vertical

The tool	What it looks like	What it does
wrench	a stick with a C or an O (or both) at either end	tightens or loosens a nut or bolt
pliers	industrial-size tweezers	bends wire, grasps small objects, or pulls out nails
wrecking bar	a small crowbar with a fork at one end and a curve at the other	breaks, separates, or otherwise mutilates wood and other materials

Bring on the Wrecking Ball!

As much as your son will love stacking his blocks, LEGOs, and Lincoln Logs, the *best* part of these endeavors is invariably the moment when he (thunderously and with astonishing force) knocks his masterpiece to smithereens. What's the deal? He feels powerful causing such calamity, and the subsequent deafening crash is a big extra smear of icing on his blown-to-bits cake. The desire to destroy doesn't mean he's destined to work in demolition; it just means he's a *boy*. It'll start innocently enough:

> **You: "Look at the pretty sand castle I built for you!"**

> **Him: Thump. (Raucous laughter as he stomps it into oblivion.)**

Your job, Mom, is to go with the flow, to laugh or clap louder than he does when the blocks come tumbling down—and to try as hard as you can not to mention the crazy mess it's making. The more you can assuage his urge to annihilate in controlled, creative ways, the less likely he will be to unleash his energies through less desirable activities.

Some constructive destruction ideas:

- Rinse and save empty soda or soup cans, and then stack them pyramid-style in the driveway (or on any other hard, smooth surface). Pretend you're bowling and take turns rolling a ball into the pyramid. Knock them all down and you win; loser has to reset the cans.

• Get an old wine cork, a plastic bottle, some vinegar and baking soda and head outside. Sprinkle a little baking soda into the bottle, pour in some vinegar and quickly plug it with the cork. Set it down in a wide-open spot and run for cover. The resulting *pop* will cement your position as the coolest mom on the planet.

• Collect old plates or decorative tiles (you can pick them up cheap at thrift stores), and place them in an old pillow case. Give him the hammer and let him take a few solid thwacks. Dump out the pieces and glue to a photo frame or garden stepping stone for the perfect homemade grandparent gift.

• Surf around YouTube for electrifying videos of ruins-in-progress. Just type in the word "demolition" and within seconds, he can be watching dozens of buildings come crashing down. Be sure to dust off a space on the mantle for the Mom of the Year trophy you just earned.

Goodness Snakes!

Their slithery, hissing, reptilian bodies might make you squirm, but to your would-be herpetologist (aka snake expert), nothing's more fascinating. He'll want to hunt for them, hold them, and possibly even house one in an enormous screen-covered tank in his bedroom. (Go ahead and shudder.) The possibility of danger is only part of the fascination. There's the way-cool shedding of the skin, the thousands of species names to memorize, and of course, the opportunity to see the food chain in glorious, gory action. ("Mom, look how the little mouse just *disappears*!")

Thankfully, most zoos have a reptile exhibit (and your town is likely home to at least one "reptile guy" who can come with several creepy friends to birthday parties), so you may be able to get away without having to own your own boa. Still, by learning a little about the suborder *Serpentes*, you'll show him you're too courageous to cower in the presence of a predator.

Fast snake facts

- Reptiles are cold-blooded animals that raise their body temperature by lying in the sun or lower it by crawling into the shade.

- There are more than 2,900 species of snakes in the world. (Only about 15 percent of them are venomous. Relieved?)

- Snakes cannot live in places like Antarctica where the ground stays frozen year-round.

(Not exactly a reason to live on the ice, but good to know!)

- Some islands, including Ireland and New Zealand, do not have snakes at all.

- The shedding of skin is technically called *ecdysis* (pronounced *EK-duh-sis*, but more commonly known as *moulting*). Young snakes shed their skins completely up to four times a year; older snakes may only shed once or twice a year.

- The king cobra generally has the reputation of being the longest (up to 18 feet) and deadliest snake in the world. Fortunately, most king cobras reside in India. Three words: God bless America.

Can you stomach it?

Even if you nearly lost your lunch when you had to dissect that poor, helpless frog back in anatomy class, now that you have a son, you're going to have to strengthen those stomach muscles (and we're not talking about that evasive six-pack). Here, an easy-for-the-queasy illustration of a snake's innards. You know, in case you were interested.

heart

stomach

Isn't That Super?

Spider-Man, Superman, Batman, and their cohorts were around when *you* were a kid. Surprised that old-school superheroes can still captivate? Just consider the undeniable and enduring appeal: superheroes are powerful, clever, handsome, and invincible. They have huge muscles, mysterious double-lives, *and* their own capes. They never have to clean their rooms and have no discernable bed-time. Lots of the time they can fly, stretch their limbs to epic lengths, perform ridiculous feats of bravery, and sometimes even make themselves invisible. They always get the bad guy (and usually the damsel-in-distress to boot, but he's probably not too interested in that . . . yet).

On top of all this, superhero comics invariably feature violent explosions (Pow! Kablam!), deafening crashes (Boom! Shazam!), and the danger and drama of a villain who *must be stopped*. The lure of the legend is obvious: superheroes are everything your son hopes to become.

Want to be a savvy Supermom? Try one of these:

Give him super style: Take an old pillowcase and pin or sew two ends together around his neck, cape-style. Just be sure to remind him that he can't *really* fly, no matter how realistic his outfit looks.

Get in the game: Take turns fantasizing about which superpower you'd choose if you could have only one. Invisibility? Telepathy? Superhuman strength? X-ray vision? The ability to blink and have dinner appear on the table? (Hey, a mom can dream, too.)

Super-family factoid to stash away for a rainy day: In the original Superman story, the Man of Steel was born Kal-El on the planet Krypton. He was rocketed to Earth as an infant by his father just moments before Krypton was destroyed. He landed in Kansas and was adopted by a farm family, who raised him as Clark Kent.

Surf *this* web: Spider-Man (aka Peter Parker) was the first teenage superhero.

Show him there actually *is* something older than you: Comic strips have been collected in hardcover book form since as early as 1833. The first one published in English was *The Adventures of Obadiah Oldbuck* (catchy name, no?) in 1842.

Brush up on your super-smarts with this handy guide to who's who (and who does what) in the world of superheroes:

The super-hero	The alias(es) or alter ego(s)	The superpower
Batman	Bruce Wayne	None per se; Batman fights crime using his innately superior scientific knowledge, detective skills, and athletic prowess.
Captain America	Steve Rogers	The pinnacle of "human perfection" after being chosen as the two-legged guinea pig to test Super-Soldier Serum. (Which, by the way, automatically regenerates in his body, rendering him eternally young.)
Doctor Druid	Anthony Ludgate Druid	Proficient in all of the basic mind-bending skills including telepathy, hypnosis, and ESP.

The super-hero	The alias(es) or alter ego(s)	The superpower
Green Lantern	Alan Scott, Hal Jordan, Kyle Rayner, John Stewart, Guy Gardner . . .	Keeper of the magical (and self-explanatory) "ring of power."
Iceman	Robert "Bobby" Louis Drake	Can freeze anything— including his own body. (One of the more lame superpowers, if you ask us.)
The Flash	Jay Garrick, Barry Allen, Wallace Rudolph "Wally" West	The dude is really fast. Crazy fast. To the point of violating basic laws of physics.
The Incredible Hulk	Robert Bruce Banner	Huge, strong, and shreds his own pants over and over to great comic effect.
Spider-Man	Peter Parker	Can cling to walls, is extremely strong, and has a sixth "spider sense" that alerts him to danger.

The super-hero	The alias(es) or alter ego(s)	The superpower
Superman	Clark Kent	"Faster than a speeding bullet, more powerful than a locomotive, and able to leap tall buildings in a single bound." (Memorize this; there may be a quiz.)
Aquaman	Orin or Arthur Curry (adopted name)	Is able to breathe under water, see and hear in the dark, and communicate with sea creatures.

Girly cues

Although your son may not be drawn to Wonder Woman on his own, feel free to enlighten him about some of her killer skills: the celebrated superbabe can ride on air currents as if flying, speak every language on the planet, and engage in hand-to-hand combat. She's also got telepathic powers, a pair of indestructible bracelets, *and* an invisible plane. Take *that*, Iceman.

Where's the Fire?

You see big, shiny, red fire trucks all the time— but have you ever really given much thought to how they work or how wondrous they really are? If your son has any say in the matter (and we're here to tell you that he will), you'll be an expert before you know it. Fire engines share several important similarities with many of the other gadgets and gizmos that will flip his little switch: They're loud. They're fast. They have lots of complicated parts.

They're often found at the scene of a fascinating disaster, where they've rushed in—sirens wailing—to save the day.

At your son's urging, you'll follow fire engines because he'll need to see them in action. You'll visit fire stations. You'll stop firefighters on the street to say "thank you" (and get teary-eyed when they tousle his little head). You'll fork over the dough for the $2,000 backyard play structure because it has the fire pole that the less expensive models don't. You'll travel the virtual world trying to find a realistic-looking fire hat for his Halloween costume, or the friendliest crew to make a surprise appearance at his birthday party. Oh, and sure hope you like dogs . . . because his relentless Dalmatian demands (they *are* the official fire dog and all) may eventually wear you down.

In the meantime, master these terms and you'll show him that Mom's on fire when it comes to flame facts:

- **AERIAL TRUCK:** a fire engine mounted with a hydraulically powered ladder that can reach up to 200 feet

- **BACKDRAFT:** an explosion that occurs when oxygen (air) reaches an oxygen-deprived fire

- **CODE ONE:** an engine traveling without lights or sirens

- **CODE THREE:** an engine traveling *with* lights and sirens (interestingly and inexplicably, there's no such thing as a standard "Code Two")

- **DECK GUN:** a large water nozzle attached to an engine that can deliver greater quantities of water than a hand-held hose

- **DRAFTING:** pulling water from a source other than an engine or hydrant, such as a lake, pond, pool, or cistern

- **GPM:** gallons per minute (as in "How many GPM are we using to put out this fire?"), the most important acronym for a firefighter

- **LDH:** nickname for a Large Diameter Hose (generally 5 inches), used when a great volume of water is needed

- **PLUG:** slang for fire hydrant, a remnant from the days when water mains actually had plugs in the top

- **QUINT:** an engine that can perform five major fire-fighting functions: carry water, pump water, have operational hoses, contain an aerial device, and house ground ladders

Try it together

Practice some of this fireman lingo together and then test it out in a sentence the next time you pass a fire engine or hydrant:

- "Hey Jack, how many GPMs do you suppose that quint can pump?"

- "Here comes a Code Three! I bet they have an LDH on board!"

- "Did you see what that poodle just did to that plug?"

What's Bugging You?

If it creeps and crawls and has the ability to send you scampering for the nearest swatter, your little love-bug is probably enamored of it. Don't blame the innocent little butterfly-and-bumblebee mobile above his crib—his sister could have the same one and he's still far more apt to ask for an ant farm for his fifth birthday. Part of it is primal; on some level he's wired for the hunt. You didn't think that would *start* with woolly mammoths, did you?

He's easing into the role, beetle by beetle. Start saving those empty mayo jars now, Mom, because you'll be making hundreds of bug-catchers over the next decade.

Note: If you're even a tiny bit squeamish about insects, you could unwittingly enhance his interest even more—by making him feel strong and brave by comparison. (This however *can* come in handy when he's old enough to operate a Bug Vac.) Try to share his enthusiasm, even as your skin goes all goose-pimply. Fostering a love of science and exploration now could be the first step on his path to a Nobel Prize, which—it's worth noting—has a cash value of more than 1.5 *million* bucks. Just saying.

He's pestering you to talk pests—again? Delight him with these creature-features:

- The life expectancy of a fly is anywhere from eight days to a year.

- Ants don't sleep.

- A pair of flies can produce more than a million offspring in just eight weeks.

- Aphids are born pregnant.

- No two spider webs in the world are the same.

- The adult female is the only blood-sucking mosquito (they need the protein to produce and feed eggs).

- Honeybees kill more people around the world than all venomous snakes combined.

- Only adult male crickets can chirp.

- Six billion dust mites happily call the average bed "home."

- And last—but certainly not least: a cockroach can live for up to a week without a head. (Ewwwwwww!)

Fun, cubed

Pick up some plastic flies or bugs (party stores sell them) and drop one into each compartment of an ice cube tray, fill with water, and freeze. Watch in delight as he plays the same prank over and over ("Is that a *bug* in your lemonade?") on Dad, Grandma, babysitters, and anyone else who stops by.

FYI

A spider is *not* an insect. It's an arachnid. The difference? See the following chart.

Insects . . .	Arachnids . . .
have three body parts	have two body parts
have six legs	have eight legs
sometimes have wings	never have wings
have one pair of eyes	can have multiple eyes
sport antennae	do not sport antennae

Creep-free ways
to enjoy insects from afar

Watch the animated Disney/Pixar flick *A Bug's Life* together (featuring an all-star cast that includes Julia Louis-Dreyfus, Phyllis Diller, Kevin Spacey, Denis Leary, and Hayden Panettiere). Serve "ants on a log" (celery or carrot sticks smeared with peanut butter and topped with raisins), drink "bug juice" (Kool-Aid, lemonade, or any concoction of your/his choosing), and enjoy.

Wheel Genius

You're not even sure of the exact make and model of your minivan—but within a few short years, your kid may be able to take apart that car's engine, distinguish a British make from a Japanese one, *and* recite the critical laundry list of differences between the '63 Corvette and the '64. (The earlier model had a split rear window and fake hood vents, by the way; the next year featured a single rear window and no vents. Oh yeah, and the '64 was a *much* quieter ride.) He'll collect Hot Wheels, beg you to procure pit passes to any

NASCAR event, and memorize every line in the animated movie *Cars*. And we won't even mention the souped-up ride he'll have his heart set on in 12 or so years.

Whereas a vehicle to you likely is simply a means of transport, think about the allure from a kid's perspective: cars are colorful, fast, loud, and powerful. They don't just take him from Point A to Point B; in his perfect little world, they do it in roaring, hair-ruffling style. This is the image that inevitably gets his engine humming, even if you'd prefer the windows all up, all the time. Yes, you might sacrifice a few blowouts over the years, but the first time he slides under your rig and changes the oil for you, it'll all have been worthwhile.

When he's driving you batty with car questions ("What does a piston do again, Mom?"), open up this can of vehicular trivia on him:

- In 1896, the Duryea (*not* the Model T, as many believe) became the first vehicle produced in quantity in the United States. Thirteen of them rolled off the lines that year.

- The "Curved Dash" Oldsmobile debuted in 1901 as the first truly mass-produced automobile. Olds made a whopping 425 of them—at a retail cost of $650 a pop.

- Before January 1, 1968, car manufacturers could decide whether or not to install seatbelts in their vehicles.

- The first traffic signal was installed in Cleveland in 1914. A traffic officer actually sat in a nearby booth and operated the green and red lights.

- The best-selling car of all time is the Toyota Corolla. The Japanese car giant has cranked out more than 35 million Corollas in just over 40 years.

- The current "record number of people" inside a microscopic Mini Cooper is . . . 21. (Hope none of them ate beans before climbing in.)

Past-pop culture bonus

In case your son is into retro TV some day, you should know that officers Starsky and Hutch drove a Ford Gran Torino (models ranged from 1974 to 1976), and that KITT, the way-cool talking car driven by Michael Knight (aka *Knight Rider*), was a 1982 Pontiac Firebird Trans Am. The name KITT? Stands for Knight Industries Two Thousand. Tossing that nugget casually into a conversation will make his engine purr.

Keep on Truckin'

Wheels are like birthday presents: the more the better! Therefore, be prepared to see your living room transformed into a parking lot jam-packed with big rigs. Your son will collect them, name them, and become intimately familiar with all of their unique capabilities and designs. In particular he'll adore the models he can fill with his own loot, so he can pretend to transport it across the imaginary miles. There's just something invitingly, irresistibly masculine about a massive rig, and the thought of manning one all by his little old lonesome is powerful imaginative play. You can't fight it, Mom, so you might as well muster up some enthusiasm.

Note to headache-prone parents: many model 18-wheelers feature an appealing (at least, to him) selection of cacophonous sounds and sirens, so if you're the one doing the purchasing, you might want to hunt down a battery-free model—or at least one with a volume control. Oh, and before you hit the stores, you'd better check the available balance on your credit card. Some of the higher-end trailer replicas—and yes, we're talking toys here—can run upwards of $500. *Each.*

Once you find a reasonably-priced model, together you'll explore all of the exciting intricacies of the home replica. When you're on the road, keep him occupied by scouting for different makes and models and impress him with your vast and comprehensive knowledge of the towering trucks beside you. (And go ahead and pump your arm and try to get the occasional driver to blow his horn. You know you want to.)

Here's some cool truck trivia to know and share:

- Although many people incorrectly refer to all big rigs generically as "semis," a *semitrailer* is technically the type that has a detachable end that rests on a separate truck bed. The obvious name for the all-in-one unit is a full trailer.

- Eighteen-wheelers get, on average, an unimpressive 4 to 6 miles per gallon. (Why nobody's bothered making a hybrid model remains a mystery.)

- The legal weight limit for an 18-wheeler is 80,000 pounds. (The average passenger car, in comparison, weighs less than 3,500 pounds.)

- Big rigs come in all lengths, but standard is about 70 to 80 feet. This probably explains why you see very few 18-wheelers parallel parked.

- A typical big rig features 10 forward gears and 2 for reverse—although some have as many as 18 gears.

- When the cab is driving without the trailer attached, it's called "bobtailing."

- Eighteen-wheelers have five axles. (What exactly they do is anyone's guess. Ask your son!)

- It takes the length of two football fields to bring an 18-wheeler going 55 miles per hour to a complete stop.

- Double tires are called "tandems." Tandems serve as a backup in the event of a blowout.

- The most common big rig manufacturers are Peterbilt, Freightliner, Kenworth, Volvo, Mack, and Western Star.

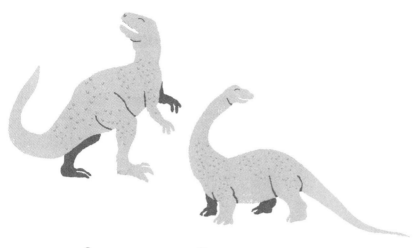

Dino-size Me!

If you acquired the bulk of your dino-data by watching *The Flintstones* (remember good old Dino?), it's time to bone up on your paleontology. Despite their annoyingly similar (and impossible to spell) names, dinosaurs are pretty cool when you think about it. They were the planet's dominant vertebrate animal for over 160 million years—that's longer than *Guiding Light* was on the air, even—and now they're totally gone. Wiped out. Extinct. And frankly, if they weren't, would any of us even know the word "extinct"? Think about it.

What's the appeal of the prehistoric in our post-modern world? The mere fact that dinosaurs don't exist any longer makes them instantly alluring. (Sigh. Even *dinosaurs* couldn't escape the postmortem popularity phenomenon.) Many of them were scaly and imposing—making them the closest thing to a real dragon your wee one can imagine. Knowing all about them allows him to use impressive terms like "pterodactyl," "stegosaurus," and "triceratops"—and he feels as tall as a T-Rex when he can pronounce these big, grown-up words (and correct your attempts, too).

Your son surely will hoard dinosaur books by the dozen, so soon enough you'll be able to wax poetic about the periods during which they lived (Triassic, Jurassic, Vlasic . . . wait, that's a pickle) and note the distinguishing difference between the meat-eating Allosaurus and the vegetarian Apatosaurus. You'll probably have to assemble a plastic skeleton replica at least once, and if you see a good price on a gently used *Jurassic Park* DVD, you might as well pick it up now.

In the meantime, devour these fossil facts and hopefully your son will never call you a *dorkosaurus*:

- The word *dinosaur* comes from a combination of the two Greek words for "terrible" and "lizard."

- Scientists studying footprints have estimated the fastest dinosaur speed to be about 27 miles per hour.

- The most complete fossilized remains of a T-Rex (dubbed "Tinker") were found in South Dakota in 1998.

- According to several sources, the largest dinosaurs were over 100 feet long and up to 50 feet tall. The smallest dinosaurs were about the size of a chicken (no word on what they tasted like).

- No one knows exactly how many dinosaur species existed . . . but the estimates range from 250 to more than 1,300.

- Scientists now believe that birds actually evolved from dinosaurs (which would make dinosaurs technically not extinct . . . right?).

Brushing up on your Latin will give you an instant understanding of many dinosaurs' distinguishing features and characteristics. Here's a handy cheat sheet:

The prefix	What it means
apato	deceptive
bronto	thunder
cera	horned
hadro	large
micro	small
nycho	clawed
pachy	thick
proto	first

The prefix	What it means
raptor	thief
rex	king
stego	roof
veloci	speedy

Give him a belly-sore-us with these silly dino-jokes

What do you call a dinosaur that destroys everything in its path?

A Tyrannosaurus Wrecks!

What kind of dinosaur can jump higher than a house?

All of them. A house can't jump!

What does a triceratops sit on?

Its tricerabottom.

What do you get when a dinosaur sneezes?

Out of the way.

Why did the dinosaur cross the road?

Because the chicken hadn't been invented yet.

Of course, no discussion of dinosaurs would be complete without a mention of Barney, the plush purple T-Rex who has achieved great fame on PBS. Yes, he's more than a little annoying . . . but a study by Yale researchers Jerome and Dorothy Singer concluded that "preschoolers who were exposed to *Barney & Friends* and a follow-up teaching activity for two weeks increased their test performance on 17 of 18 questions reflecting facts of readiness-to-learn skills." So stock the TiVo and feel good about it—even if you have to leave the room.

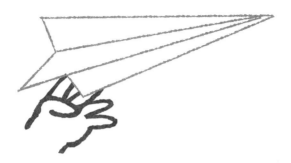

Weird Science

Until this very moment in time, you may never have questioned, for instance, what makes magnets attract or how electricity works. As far as lots of folks are concerned, they do, it does, enough said. Your son, however, may not be satisfied with the mere fact of a thing's existence. From a simple pencil sharpener to the most sophisticated of machines, he'll want to know how it works, why it works, and what all of its many and myriad parts are called. If it plugs in, winds up, twirls about, or features pulsating lights, demure beeps, deafening sirens, or more parts than a jigsaw puzzle the size of Paris, all the better.

Smart as you may be, there could come a time when you find yourself unable to satisfy some or all of his many curiosities: How do batteries work? What's that little thingy inside a light bulb for? Where does all of that information on your computer *live*? How does gas make the car go? How can an X-ray machine take a picture of the *inside* of your body? Where does static electricity come from? And *how*, for the love of kryptonite, can airplanes fly when people can't?

Sure, you could go back to school full-time until you know everything about everything. Or you can save yourself a lot of time and effort by picking up a copy of *How Things Work*, a useful, illustrated handbook that picks up where Mom and Dad's schooling may have left off (or frankly, became a little fuzzy). Kid's got an urgent query and you can't find the answer in there? Log onto www.howstuffworks.com, and type in a search term. Within seconds, the site's search engine will demystify everything from how dye changes the color of your hair to precisely what causes those pesky ice cream headaches. (The cold triggers a nerve center on the roof of your mouth, causing the blood vessels in your head to dilate. The solution? Keep frozen treats off the roof of your mouth! Eureka!)

Here are some fun science experiments you can do together to explore the world (without blowing it up):

- **Homemade Mount St. Helens:** Place an empty 2-liter soda bottle on a cookie sheet or piece of plywood. This will be the inside of your volcano; you can create the mound around it—depending on how crafty you are—with wadded-up newspaper and tape or go full-tilt with papier-mâché. Then in a cup mix together 1 tablespoon of liquid dish soap, 1 tablespoon of baking soda, and a few drops of red food coloring, and pour the mixture into the empty bottle. (If you're not already outside, this is a good time to get there.) Pour $\frac{1}{4}$ cup of vinegar into the bottle and watch your volcano erupt!

- **Plane and simple:** Nothing like whipping up a 30-second paper airplane to get him interested in aerospace engineering. (Although obviously they vary greatly, paper airplanes and actual multi-ton jetliners rely on the very same principles to stay airborne.) Help him craft his aircraft, and then keep track of its longest flight, best nose-dive, and highest lift-off.

- **Groovy, baby!** Make your very own lava lamp by mixing some water and baby oil ($1/4$ to $3/4$ ratio) with a few drops of food coloring in a plastic bottle. Close the lid tightly and watch as the "lava" bubbles and blobs about, taking the opportunity to explain that the water and the oil won't mix because water has greater density than oil. (This experiment may conjure up some hazy dorm-room memories; feel free to keep these to yourself.)

Insider tip

Many boys never really outgrow this fascination with how things work (hence your hubby's cluttered closet/garage/workshop), so the sooner you accept his lust for gear, gadgets, and gizmos, the better. Sure, you'll sacrifice a few towels to the rag pile over the years, but there probably will be some no-cost home repairs in it for you somewhere down the line.

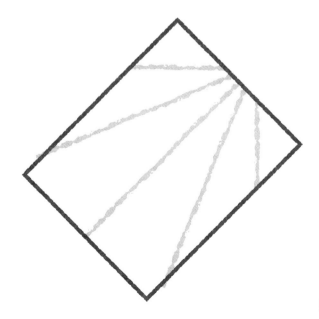

Soldier On!

Remember when pampered Private Benjamin got to boot camp and wondered where all the yachts and condos were? Well, your son's image of military life probably will be a lot less glamorous. He'll love suiting up in his fatigues and practicing tricky maneuvers like the belly-crawl-through-the-mud and the see-how-fast-I-can-scale-the-fence. Naturally, navigating the living room's latest obstacle course will be a daily drill. And yes, he will come to covet toy guns, whether you like it or not (and we're guessing, probably not).

Before he sees his first recruitment ad, he'll understand—inexplicably—a few basics: Serving his country is an act of bravery. It's scary (in a good way). It's dangerous. You get to carry weapons! Fly helicopters. Drive tanks. Jump out of airplanes. Yell commands. And the outfits are *really freaking macho*.

You only have to visit a park or playground once to see that soldier-worship is a natural phase most boys will go through at one point or another. Of course, you'll worry about encouraging this and you'll agonize over whether to give him the toy bazooka he wants more than anything else for his birthday. Are you condoning violence? Promoting weaponry? Glamorizing war?

At ease, Mom. This is just another proverbial hat he'll want to try on—for fun and exploration, period. Playing "army guys" is rough-and-tumble fun at its finest, so give him the green light to play G.I. Joe when the urge strikes. (Remember, as soon as anything is utterly "off-limits," its appeal only escalates.) Learn a little armed forces lingo and *you'll* be a force to be reckoned with:

- **AHA:** ammunition holding area

- **ANT HILL:** combat outpost with a multitude of visible radio antennae

- **BEER THIRTY:** scheduled time of dismissal from duties (works in civilian life, too—although feel free to change it to wine-o'clock if you prefer)

- **BLUES:** military dress uniform

- **COMMANDO:** a hit-and-run unit used for surprise attacks (and *you* thought it only meant forgetting your underpants!)

- **CP:** command post

- **DEUCE-AND-A-HALF:** two-and-a-half ton military vehicle

- **FULL BIRD:** colonel (whose insignia is an eagle)

- **HALF BIRD:** the lower-ranked lieutenant colonel

- **LIMA CHARLIE:** code for communication has been received "loud and clear" (from the NATO phonetic alphabet)

- **MOONBEAM:** flashlight

- **MRE:** vacuum-sealed military meal (Meal Ready to Eat)

- **OSCAR MIKE:** NATO code for "on the move"

- **QUARTERS:** housing

- **RACK:** bed

- **S/F:** abbreviation for *Semper Fidelis* (Latin for "always faithful"), used as a closing salutation in letters

- **WILCO:** shorthand for "will comply"

- **ZOOMIE:** pilot

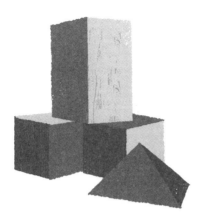

Chip Off the Old Block

While no one would dare suggest that building blocks appeal to one sex over the other, stackable toys tend to remain a favorite of little boys long after their sisters have moved on to paper dolls and fairy wands. From LEGOs to Lincoln Logs to that beloved box of wooden shapes that Grandpa sanded in his workshop those many decades ago, if he can stack them, create elaborate fortresses out of them, and, yes, knock them down with great, thunderous force, you can expect to be tripping over them for years to come.

Children may be naturally drawn to blocks, but they're certainly not aware of the benefits of their toy building materials. Carrying, sorting, and moving the pieces around actually helps build small muscles. Lining them up aids in the development of his hand-eye coordination. Stacking them vertically teaches him about balance. And of course, when you ask him to build something—a bridge or a house, for instance—he has to rely on his knowledge of these things. ("A house usually has a pointy roof!" "Drawbridges go up and then come back down!") Home schooling starts *now*.

Here are some things about blocks you may not know: There's no such thing as too many. Bigger isn't necessarily better. It hurts *really* badly if you step on one and it lodges into the soft underbelly of your arch. For the last reason in particular, now's a good time to learn the old clean-up song: "Clean up, clean up, everybody everywhere! Clean up, clean up, everybody do their share!" Belting out a spirited rendition of this tune when it's time to stash the stackables may just save your sole(s).

A quick word about one of today's hottest blocks: Remember those primary-colored, decidedly chunky, clickable bricks of your youth? Well, they still make LEGOs, but your son will probably move past those pretty early in the game. Today LEGO makes all manner of kits that kids can use to craft helicopters, race cars, beach houses, tarantulas, even dinosaurs—all out of hundreds (or even thousands) of eensy, weensy little pieces. A collection of sci-fi LEGO beings that are part-organic, part-machine, called Bionicles, are a universal favorite. They have stories, plots, heroes, adventures, and lots and lots of licensed merchandise. Bionicles also have their very own written language made up of the Matoran alphabet (which looks a lot like gang graffiti but really isn't, honest). Each symbol in this make-believe language corresponds with a particular letter of the alphabet. Master it, and you can write to each other in code. (Yeah, in your spare time.)

The good news: the Bionicle kits come with step-by-step picture instructions. The bad news: the instruction booklets can be fatter than the New York City phone book. The great news: these kits will delight and entertain him for hours at a stretch. The you-decide-if-it's-good-or-bad news: he may very well need a foreman (and yes, that'll likely be you) to execute the finished product. Sign up for the job, and it'll keep him out of trouble.

Cool Mom opportunity

After every block-building extravaganza, take pictures of his creations and put them into an album designated for just this purpose. This is a great way to track his building progress and memorialize his finest designs. Plus the photo memory of the accomplishment might make it easier to convince him to pack up the blocks when clean-up time rolls around.

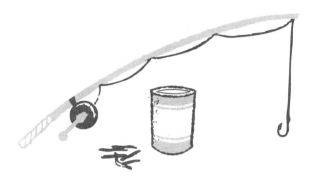

Go Fish!

When your hubby says he's "going fishing," you're probably not too far off the mark by translating this into "going to get up at an ungodly hour to go sit around and drink beer all day with the boys while fish nibble on the free snacks one of us will have attached to the ends of our lines." (Or something similar.) For many men, fishing is about hanging out, tuning out, and bonding with buddies. If they happen to actually land something scaly while they're at it, all the better.

For your little fisherman, the lure (so to speak) is simple: to catch something, he's got to outsmart it. If he succeeds, he's got tangible (wriggling, writhing, possibly even edible) evidence of his prowess. This last bit alone probably is enough to bait him—hook, line, and sinker.

Learn a few trolling terms and you'll show him Mom's a master of the art of angling (that's just another word for fishing). Don't worry; you can't go overboard with these:

- **BARB:** the little nick on the back side of a fish hook, intended to prevent the fish from "backing off" of the bait

- **BOATED:** term for a fish that's been caught and brought on board

- **GUIDES:** the little loops on a fishing rod that the line goes through

- **HIT:** the moment when the fisherman feels the fish on the line; also known as a "bump" or a "strike"

- **HULL:** the outside bottom part of a boat

- **PFD:** Personal Flotation Device (you know, a life vest)

- **SINKER:** a weight tied to the fishing line to drag the bait into deeper water—where the *big* fish hang out

- **STICK:** slang for fishing rod

- **TACKLE:** all of the copious fishing gear combined

Ahoy, Mates!

By definition, *piracy* refers to any criminal acts committed at sea (or, interestingly, in the air—although no famous sky-pirates spring to mind). Pirates are famous for pillaging, kidnapping, murdering, and all manner of dastardly crimes in between. But don't let that daunt you! It's not the violence your son will be drawn to so much as the mystery and adventure. (Wooden legs and missing eyeballs are pretty cool, too.) Blame Robert Lewis Stevenson's *Treasure Island* and J. M. Barrie's *Peter Pan* (remember good old Captain Hook?)

for planting the seed—and thank the Disney folks for casting Johnny Depp as Captain Jack Sparrow in *Pirates of the Caribbean*, thereby making this one pirate flick you won't mind watching over and over. And over and over.

Expect your son to occasionally hobble about (wooden legs don't bend like the flesh kind), stretch one sleeve of his shirt to ungodly lengths (to disguise the hand holding the "hook"), and to insist on wearing an eye patch. Yes, in public.

Like his other temporary obsessions, this one will blow over eventually. In the meantime, between the Johnny Depp thing and the fact that the whole skull-and-crossbones look is still *très chic*, it's really not that hard to embrace your inner buccaneer.

Mark your calendar

September 19 is International Talk Like a Pirate Day (for real). To celebrate, round up all your mates and bust out your best *arrrrghs* . . . and see who can run with it the longest. This mini-glossary of terms will have you talking the talk:

- **AHOY:** "Hi there!"

- **AVAST:** "Halt!"

- **AYE:** "I totally agree."

- **AYE-AYE:** "I'll get right on it."

- **BILGE:** the lowest, and least desirable, part of a ship

- **BOOTY:** loot, haul

- **DAVY JONES'S LOCKER:** the bottom of the sea

- **GANGWAY:** "Get out of my way!"

- **GROG:** any type of (alcoholic) drink except beer

- **LUBBER:** short for "land lubber" (lover) or non-sailor

- **ME HARDIES:** my friends or crew

- **SMARTLY:** ASAP

- **WENCH:** woman

A sample script to consider

You: "Avast, mate!"

Son: "Whatcha want, me hardy?"

You: "That room of yours is a bilge."

Son: "Aye."

You: "Well, get her cleaned, smartly!"

Son: "Aye-aye."

You: "Anything that's not picked up will wind up in Davy Jones's locker."

Son: "Gangway, you saucy wench! Er, *please*."

Book it

Even tender-aged pirates can enjoy classic tales like *Treasure Island*. Look for special "young reader" editions and edit as you read if necessary. Or, ease into things with more juvenile titles like *What If You Met a Pirate?* or *Do Pirates Take Baths?*

Get in the Sling

In little boy land, the only thing cooler than hurtling rocks and other small bits into space is any piece of equipment that helps you launch them farther, faster, and hopefully, with something resembling accuracy. If you've never wielded a sling-shot before, you're actually missing out. These sometimes crude tools (a forked branch and a rubber band are all you really need) can be great fun—as long as you have a modicum of coordination. If not, protective eyewear is suggested. In fact, the eyewear isn't a bad idea in general, regardless of your slinging skills.

Also known as a shanghai, catapult, or katty, a sling-shot features a Y-shape frame with a length of rubber attached to the two prongs; the long base of the Y is the handle. To work one, hold the handle in your non-dominant hand, and place a rock or other projectile in the saddle or center of the rubber piece. Now extend the arm holding the handle until it is totally straight, and pull the projectile back toward you until the rubber is taut. Close your eyes, say a little prayer, and release. In a perfect world, the rock will shoot *away* from you in a lovely arc. (In a slightly less ideal scenario, you'll release at just the wrong moment, get your fingers painfully snapped by the band, and the rock will pop and spin and finally bounce off of your temple.)

Some advice: *practice, practice, practice.*

"But I don't want my son to have one of these dangerous, deadly contraptions!" you may be thinking.

And frankly, the sling-shot does sometimes get a bad rap. In fact, just about every mischievous pop culture lad—from Dennis the Menace to Bart Simpson—has had a not-so-fortuitous run-in with one. Nevertheless, eventually your son will get one as a gift, find one at a friend's house, or fashion one from easy-to-find materials lying about. Hence, the importance of establishing one important ground rule before engaging in play:

*Sling shots are never meant to be a weapon
or tool of destruction,
and therefore must always and forever
be pointed away from people,
pets, windows, and anything else
living, breathing, or even the slightest
bit fragile.*

You can encourage proper use of this gizmo by setting up (inanimate) targets for him to shoot at, preferably outside in a wide-open space. A stack of empty soda or soup cans works great for this.

Be a big shot and make your own

Find a sturdy, Y-shape stick between 6 and 12 inches long. If it's rough, peeling some of the bark away from the handle will make holding it more comfortable. Next, hunt down a long, thick rubber band, a bicycle inner tube, or some surgical tubing (available at medical supply stores). Take a small scrap of leather, about two inches by four inches (you can cut the tongue out of an old leather shoe if you don't have a scrap handy), and use an X-Acto knife to cut a slit in each of the two shorter ends; this will form the saddle or basket. If you are using a rubber band, cut it in half and thread it through the holes. (Any sort of tubing can just get threaded without cutting.) Use smaller rubber bands to *tightly* secure each end of your stretchy material to either of the two prongs on your stick. The leather saddle should be exactly in the center to ensure a straight shot, and there should be enough slack in the band or tubing to get some momentum going. Now just slip on your protective eyewear, find a rock, line up your target, and take aim!

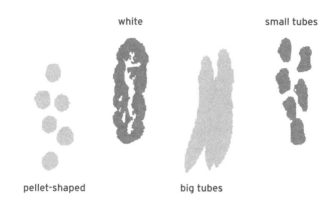

white

small tubes

pellet-shaped

big tubes

The Scoop on Poop

While there's a good chance that your son will be enamored of his own bodily waste, it may be animal droppings—officially known as *scat*—that turn out to have even greater allure. Sleuthing around as the Sherlock Holmes of Manure is almost a rite of passage, and the mere fact that this grosses you out may be enough to solidify his seemingly unholy interest. (Do please note there is an official science—known as scatology or coprology—devoted to this delightful study.)

Rather than finding reasons to discourage your little dung detective, use his fecal fascination to help him hone his powers of deduction and observation. Scat identification isn't easy; nor is it for the lazy or weak of heart. This poo-primer will ensure a safe and productive passage through the cow pies of your future:

1. Never, ever, *ever* touch the scat. Under any circumstances. In fact, the pros suggest not even inhaling if there's a pile nearby, as some diseases can be contracted through airborne particles. Two words: stay upwind.

2. When you stumble across some droppings, take notes in a journal. Note the size, length, width, and form (is it round, tubular, ropy, flat?). Is it all in one piece or more pellet-like? What color is it? (And are we having fun yet?)

3. Don't forget to record details like time of day, features, and any relevant clues as to who the pooper might be (paw prints, etc.).

4. Draw pictures together of your findings. Gross? Maybe. But consider that Jackson Pollock was famous before he even died, and a lot of his work looks suspiciously scat-like.

5. Compare your drawings to the ones in the chart below to determine the source of your scat.

6. Silently say to yourself, "Holy crap." After all, you have to laugh. This is pretty funny stuff.

If the scat is . . .	The source could be . . .
pellet-shaped	deer, elk, llama, rabbit
blob-like	bear, cow, buffalo
big tubes	dog, coyote, goose, bobcat
small tubes	mouse, rat, bat
white	bird, reptile, amphibian

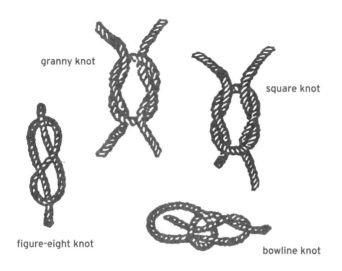

granny knot

square knot

figure-eight knot

bowline knot

Knot on Your Life

Unless you were a dedicated Girl Scout, you may live by the maxim, "If you can't tie a knot, tie a lot!" But the truth is, there are dozens of ways to join two (or more) strings together beyond your basic shoelace technique—and each serves a particular purpose. What's it to you? Knots are a critical tool in the rough-and-tumble world little boys inhabit. From tying down tents to rigging a fishing pole, there's no end to the list of tasks that demand binding skills. Help him master a few of the basics and he'll be on his way to racking up the merit badges.

When you're ready to learn the ropes, one highly recommended resource is the handy *Klutz Book of Knots*. It comes with its own strings, and each page offers a different knot to master with perforated illustrations that literally guide you through the tying process.

Check out this chart to familiarize yourself with some basic knots and their functions:

This knot . . .	Is used as . . .
granny knot	a binding knot to secure a rope around an object
hitching tie	a not-very-strong, quick-release knot to tie up all manner of things
bowline	a temporary loop at the end of a rope to secure something, as to a post
square knot	a way to connect two ropes of equal size (also known as a "reef knot")

This knot . . .	Is used as . . .
clove hitch	a means to secure lines (ropes) running along a series of posts
figure-eight	a way to stop a rope from running out of a retaining device

Reach for the Sky

Since you likely already know that your son is enamored of loud noises, it should come as no surprise that one of his all-time favorite holidays (up there with his birthday and Halloween, even) will be the star-spangled Fourth of July. A whole day dedicated to pyrotechnics? With sanctioned explosions and possibly even permission to stand next to someone who is wielding matches? It's a boy's dream come true.

Now, before you bust out the bottle rockets, it's a good idea to find out if fireworks are legal in your city, county, and state. The Consumer Product Safety Commission (CPSC.gov) has a handy list of who-can-do-what-where you might want to peruse before lighting up. Some other tips offered by the CPSC (most of which seem pretty obvious, but you really can't be too careful where explosives are concerned) include the following:

- Do not allow young children to play with fireworks under any circumstances. Sparklers, considered by many to be the ideal "safe" firework, burn at very high temperatures and can easily ignite clothing. Children cannot understand the danger involved and cannot act appropriately in case of emergency. (Remember when your mom stuck a sparkler right into each cupcake? Yeah, that's not happening anymore.)

- Light fireworks outdoors in a clear area away from houses, dry leaves or grass, and flammable materials. (Certainly you knew this.)

- Keep a bucket of water nearby for emergencies and for pouring on fireworks that don't go off. (Got that, Girl Scouts?)

- Never ignite fireworks in a container, especially a glass or metal container. (Even though it would probably look and sound very cool if you did.)

- Never have any portion of your body directly over a firework while lighting. (And if you didn't know *that* intuitively, how you made it this far in life is a great mystery.)

- Don't experiment with homemade fireworks. (Like you would!)

- Observe local laws. (A bunch of attorneys insisted that be included.)

Somewhat useless but also interesting fireworks facts

- The record for the largest firework display consisted of 66,326 fireworks and was achieved in Madeira, Portugal on New Year's Eve 2006. They're still cleaning up the debris.

- The world's longest firework waterfall appeared as part of the Ariake Seas Fireworks Festival in Fukuoka, Japan. The aptly named "Niagara Falls" measured more than 10,255 feet.

- The record for the most firework rockets launched in 30 seconds is 56,405. The stunt was pulled off by Fantastic Fireworks at the 10th British Firework Championship in Plymouth, UK, in 2006.

Boom town

Did you know that different explosions actually have different names? Blow him away next time you're watching a fireworks show by showing him Mom knows a few technical terms:

What it's called	What it looks like
brocade	a spider web–like pattern, like fine lace
chrysanthemum	a flower-like pattern
peony	a pattern of colored lights that looks like a round ball
dahlia	a starfish-like pattern
waterfall	an effect that produces long-lasting sparks, creating a waterfall-like pattern
glitter palm	a sparkling or flashing effect that form a palm tree–like pattern

Goal-
Oriented?

The first time you watch him flick a Cheerio deftly into a sideways cup, you'll realize what veteran moms of little boys have long known: anything can be a ball and a goal. His need to "score" is primal, and you can set him up for success by encouraging productive use of his athletic energies.

Keep in mind that the benefits of playing organized sports are limitless: group activities promote both fun and fitness, encourage social interaction, boost self-confidence, and teach kids valuable lessons about cooperation, graciousness, and humility. (In other words, "You win some, you lose some.")

In addition to his desire to participate in a variety of sports, he may well become an enthusiastic spectator as well. From relatively tame table tennis to rough-and-tumble rugby, if there's a program devoted to it, he's bound to want to watch it. He'll stockpile, swap, and obsess over piles of cards bearing the vital stats of his favorite players. He'll memorize names, scores, and plays, and lament the trading of key players to less desirable teams. Shin guards, shoulder pads, jockstraps, helmets, racquets, bats, clubs, cleats, sticks, paddles, pucks, birdies, and balls of every imaginable shape and size will clog every inch of your storage space. (It may lift your spirits to know that tippy-top tier pro athletes are raking in as much as 10 million bucks a year—and signing multi-year contracts. And who's the first person they always say "hi" to on camera? Yup—Mom.)

You don't have to pretend to love ESPN to show him you're a team player. Master these moves and he'll be *your* biggest fan:

- Go outside and toss a ball or a Frisbee with him. What he won't remember: your pitiful throws or fumbling, bumbling catches. What he will remember: being outside with Mom, doing something he loves to do.

- Rent a "sports flick" and watch it with him. There are plenty of great ones with actual plots that you can enjoy while he's busy getting into the game scenes. Best bets: *Rocky*, *Field of Dreams*, *Little Giants*, *A League of Their Own*, *Cool Runnings*, *The Mighty Ducks*, and, of course, the cult classic, *The Bad News Bears*.

- If (okay, *when*) he gets into organized sports, sign up to be Team Mom. She's the one that maintains the snack/drink calendar, keeps players notified of schedule changes, organizes fundraising activities . . . you know, the stuff you can do in your sleep because you do it at home every day.

• When he settles on a sport (or seven), check out momsguide.com. For just a few bucks, you can purchase laminated cheat sheets that demystify a dozen popular sports. Written by a mom for moms . . . or anyone else that feels out of his or her league on the sidelines.

Batter up!

Test your sports trivia skills and see if you're better off benched:

1. Which of these is a real rugby position?
    a. lancer
    b. hooker
    c. poacher
    d. crusher

2. Which item would you NOT see being thrown at a track and field meet?
    a. javelin
    b. discus

c. hammer

d. welly

3. What do you call a shirt worn by a British jockey?

    a. silks

    b. jumper

    c. jersey

    d. topper

4. What is the little thingy that holds a football upright before a kickoff called?

    a. kicking shoe

    b. kicking tee

    c. kick stand

    d. kick stop

5. In hockey, what is the area in front of the goal called?

    a. box

    b. loop

    c. crease

    d. circle

Answers: 1: b; 2: d; 3: a; 4: b; 5: c

Hold the Fort

To you, your living room couch is a cozy place to curl up with a nice goblet of wine and your hubby, a good friend, a juicy book, or a fantastic movie. To your son, it's a pile of pillows just *begging* to be fashioned into an elaborate fort or a fanciful castle. Likewise, a king-size top sheet and the dining room table or an old card table can keep him entertained for days.

The building of make-believe forts, foxholes, and other hideouts is one of the oldest childhood pastimes around. Consider the appeal: every-thing else in the house, it's pretty clear to your son, belongs to *you*. For a few shining minutes or hours, his self-made cave is his very own space. It's cozy in there, warm, and comforting—like a womb. It's private, secret, and safe. Best of all, it's scaled down to his size, unlike much of the rest of the world.

Sure, fort-building temporarily destroys your décor—but if you confine the mess to one room or area at a time (and insist that clean-up is part of the process), it's worth the effort. If the weather cooperates, alfresco fortresses are always a hit, too.

Some other hideout hints:

- Give him a flashlight to play with in his hide-out. He'll spend hours exploring the many visual effects he can create in there and honing his hand-puppet skills.

- Make the space extra snuggly by setting him up with a fluffy blanket, some cozy pillows, and a stack of books to peruse.

- Serve him a special surprise snack. Show him you respect his privacy by placing it on a tray and sliding it in on the sly.

- An oversized cardboard box—possible excuse to buy a new dishwasher?—makes a cool playhouse. Use a box-cutter or utility knife to cut out doors and windows, and let him paint, color, or otherwise decorate it inside and out. This is a great rainy-day project best done in the garage.

- Handy with a hammer (or know a reasonably priced handyman)? Consider springing for a tree house. Every aspiring Huck Finn—even after they have become grown men—pines for one of these. If you can afford it and have the space, a permanent play structure is a great investment.

Consider the Sorcerer

Virtually every child on earth will fantasize at one point or another about having magical powers. If you tuned into *I Dream of Jeannie* or *Bewitched* as a kid, surely you remember the bitter envy you felt when you watched these gals wiggle their noses or nod their heads and create fantastical events. When you realized you'd probably never have paranormal powers of your own, you may have spent a few summers combing beaches, hoping to stumble upon a bottled-up genie to grant wishes *for* you instead.

Similarly, when he discovers wizards, warlocks, and all of their phantasmagorical glory, expect your son to go gaga over the idea. Cloaked in his costume cape (or a pillow case pinned around his shoulders), he'll concoct potions and execute spells with dramatic flourish. As a wizard is, by definition, a "wise one," it should come as no surprise that he relishes playing this role. What child—boy or girl—wouldn't wish to know it *all*?

Where you had Tabitha and the eponymous Jeannie, the modern day magical male hero is, of course, Harry Potter. The infamously bespectacled boy is particularly alluring because, at least for a spell (pun intended), he doesn't even know he's a wizard! Talk about a happy surprise. As the Harry Potter stories aren't exactly of the early-reader variety (and the movies can be downright terrifying to young tots), it'll be a while before you're regaling him with the happenings at Hogwarts. Likewise with *The Wizard of Oz*—an undeniable classic, but still a tad on the scary side. Unless you want your son sleeping in your bed for the next several years, it may be best to hold off on these for a bit.

In the interim, smile along as he plays soothsayer, assure him that you *did* see his ears wiggle a little, and pretend to be wowed by his supernatural powers. Help him fashion a pointy hat and magic wand, and make up rhyming spells together to alter various household objects and living creatures. (Mom bonus: The things he chooses to change or wish for may surprise you—and give you some real insight into the inner workings of his mysterious boy-brain.)

This darling ditty by poet Kenn Nesbitt should shed some light on why your little dude is so absorbed with sorcery—and perhaps one day, convince him he's actually divine just as he is:

> **I'm a Wizard, I'm a Warlock**
> *I'm a wizard, I'm a warlock,*
> *I'm a wonder of the age.*
> *I'm a sorcerer, magician,*
> *prestidigitator, sage.*

I can change into a chicken,
or perhaps a purple pig.
I can wave my wand and, presto,
I'm a waffle with a wig.

With the power in my pinky
I can burst like a balloon
or transform into a tiger
with the head of a baboon.

If I wiggle on my earlobe
or I knock upon my knee
I become a dancing doughnut
or a turtle in a tree.

Just a simple incantation
and I deftly disappear,
which I never should have done
because I've been this way all year.

And despite my mighty magic
I'm impossible to see,
for I never learned the spells I need
to turn back into me.

Mummy Dearest

Wondering why mini-men are mad about mummies? Like girls and their mermaids, there is something appealing about a creature that is *kind of* human—but not. And then there's the fright factor. Think about it: you take an embalmed body, add a curse or two, throw in some good, old-fashioned fright-night tales, and you've got the makings of just the sort of gore boys are inclined to adore.

If you've never given the mummy a passing thought (and certainly no one would blame you if you hadn't), you're actually missing out on some interesting historical trivia. For instance, while mummies are usually associated with Egypt, they have been found all over the world, from Alaska to Greenland. The oldest human mummy ever discovered dates back more than 5,000 years (more than 2,000 years before the famous King Tut ambled about, if that's any point of reference). And while we typically picture the cloth-wrapped corpse when we think of a mummy, bodies can and have been preserved in ice, snow, bogs, mud, and any number of stinky chemicals.

The original idea behind intentional mummification was to preserve the body for the afterlife, which was generally assumed to parallel the present. For this reason, mummies were often entombed along with obscene hordes of riches—clearly by folks who put little faith in the phrase, "You can't take it with you." Getting in the spirit? Now get ready to share some mummy fun with your son!

That's a wrap

Take an old white sheet (you can pick one up for pennies at a thrift store if you don't have one handy) and rip it into three-inch strips. Have him wear a light colored T-shirt and shorts, as well as sneakers with white socks pulled up *over* them. Start at his ankles by tying the end of one strip into a loose knot, and wrapping upward. Use cloth tape to secure the end of each piece before starting on another section. When he's fully swathed, smear some charcoal eye shadow around his eye sockets and add a dusting of baby powder to his hair to complete the "living dead" look. With arms outstretched and a dull glaze in his eyes, help him practice his "sleep-walking" until he's mastered the move to startling effect.

Get thee to a mummery

When talk of embalmed bodies has you feeling bogged down, tickle his funny bone with these riddles:

Why are your secrets safe with a mummy?

Because they always keep things under wraps.

Do mummies like being mummies?

Of corpse!

Where do mummies like to swim?

The Dead Sea.

Why did the mummy go to the movies alone?

Because he didn't have any body to go with.

Why didn't the mummy try out for the soccer team?

He didn't have the guts.

Talk like an Egyptian

Take him on a silly Egyptian adventure with the book *Skippyjon Jones in Mummy Trouble.*

Private Lessons

No book on boys (for non-boys) would be complete without a chapter on private parts—one in particular. If you're not aware of a certain fact yet, you will be soon: little boys love their willies. (And while you are welcome to use the technical term with him from the get-go, for the purposes of not sounding like a medical manifesto, this section will stick with euphemisms.)

Here's the deal: one day in the not-too-distant future, your little guy is going to discover he's got a bewildering body part that *you* don't have—and your life will never be the same. Look at it from his point of view: he's got this really cool thing attached to his front that jiggles and squirts and flops about. Unlike any of his other appendages, it seems to have a mind of its own. It's located within convenient arm's reach at all times, so tinkering with it may prove to be irresistible. His fascination with his own anatomy will surely grow as he does, especially when he learns he can do tricks with it—like write his name in the sand or snow. (Let's see *you* do that, Mom!)

Soon enough, he'll grasp the fact that there's a *reason* they call them "private parts." In the meantime, a few . . . pointers.

To snip or not to snip

That is the (*very* personal) question. Turns out, just about half of all baby boys in the United States are circumcised, so whatever you decide, your son won't be altogether different. Parents who do opt for this procedure frequently do it for religious beliefs, concerns about hygiene, or for cultural/social motivations. Circumcised infants are less likely to develop urinary tract infections, and the area can be easier to clean. On the flip side, the procedure can be painful—and any type of surgery carries a degree of risk. Even the American Academy of Pediatrics doesn't rule in favor *or* against circumcision—instead leaving the decision entirely up to parents. All you can do is discuss it with your hubby (he's likely to feel more strongly about it than you do anyhow), weigh your options, make the call, and move on.

Standing ovation

Many a mom who's in charge of potty training will simply show her son how she does it (sitting down). This can save a lot of wipe-ups, for sure. Nevertheless, eventually he'll want to do it "like Daddy" (or brother or cousin or friend). Use these tips to keep the mess to a minimum:

- Toss some Cheerios or ice cubes into the bowl and call it target practice.

- Drip a few drops of blue food color into the bowl, and tell him that if he hits the center of the bowl the water will magically turn green. He'll be certain to watch his aim!

- Let him practice peeing outside (Oh, come on! Everybody does it!), where he can perfect his skills by shooting for rocks, leaves, and other marks.

Fiddler on the couch

It's *right there*, between his legs. Of course he's going to be curious about it. When he does repeatedly reach south of the border, never tell him it's bad or dirty. Simply explain that "private parts are for private places," then distract him with a game or activity. Repeat as necessary (this could be often), and leave it at that.

About the Author

photo by Renée Vernon

Jenna McCarthy is an internationally published writer and the author of *The Parent Trip: From High Heels and Parties to Highchairs and Potties*, and *Cheers to the New Mom!/Cheers to the New Dad!* Her work has appeared in more than 50 magazines, on dozens of Web sites, and in several anthologies, including the popular Chicken Soup series. Jenna currently is hard at work on her next project, a practical guide to living with and continuing to love the TV-addicted, listening-impaired, not-quite-handy man that you married. In her spare time, she wonders what she used to do with all of her spare time. Visit her online at www.jennamccarthy.com.